BBC
DOCTOR WHO
Flatline

A story based on the original script by
JAMIE MATHIESON

Level 3

Retold by David Maule

Series Editors: Andy Hopkins and Jocelyn Potter

Pearson Education Limited
KAO Two
KAO Park, Harlow,
Essex, CM17 9NA, England
and Associated Companies throughout the world.

ISBN: 978-1-292-20615-8
This edition first published by Pearson Education Ltd 2018
5 7 9 10 8 6

The authors have asserted their moral rights in accordance
with the Copyright Designs and Patents Act 1988
Set in 9pt/14pt Xenois Slab Pro
SWTC/05

Published by Pearson Education Limited

For a complete list of the titles available in the Pearson English Readers series, visit
www.pearsonenglishreaders.com.
Alternatively, write to your local Pearson Education office or
to Pearson English Readers Marketing Department,
Pearson Education, KAO Two, KAO Park, Harlow, Essex, CM17 9NA

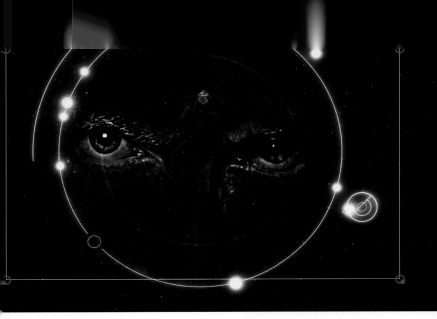

Contents

The Doctor

The Doctor is an alien, a Time Lord from Gallifrey, far away in the universe. Everyone calls him 'the Doctor'. He travels the universe, has adventures and saves people in danger. He has two hearts, and he is about 2,000 years old. When the Doctor's body becomes old or ill, he changes it for a new one. He has had many different bodies before the one in this story.

The Doctor doesn't use a gun, and tries not to kill anyone. His sonic screwdriver has many uses. It can unlock doors, use electronic devices and see inside things. He also has a plain white card – psychic paper – in a card holder. He shows it when he needs to. The reader sees on it what the Doctor wants him or her to see.

The TARDIS

The Doctor travels through time and space in a time machine called the TARDIS. On the outside, the TARDIS looks like a blue police box from Earth. These blue boxes were used in the UK, many years ago, to call the police. The inside of the TARDIS is very different. It has many rooms full of computers and machines, and is much bigger than on the outside.

The Doctor's Companion: Clara Oswald

The Doctor usually travels with someone from Earth. In this story, the Doctor's companion is Clara Oswald, an English teacher at a London school. As a companion, she is the Doctor's assistant and friend, and she helps him on his adventures. At the end of an adventure, the TARDIS returns the companion to Earth. They usually arrive back at exactly the same time as they left.

Rigsy

Rigsy is a graffiti artist and he is proud of his work, but he was caught by the police. His punishment for painting on walls is Community Payback.

Fenton

When people's crimes aren't serious, they sometimes have to do work for their town or city. This is called Community Payback. Fenton gives orders to a Community Payback group of men and watches them work.

PC Forrest

PC Forrest is a policewoman. She is quite young and hasn't done the job for very long.

Bill

Bill is a train driver. He moves empty trains around so they are in the right place for the next day.

Introduction

'Fine, I'll tell you who I am,' Clara said. She moved closer to him and spoke quietly into his ear. 'I'm your only hope of staying alive. That's who I am.'

Clara, the Doctor's companion on his travels through space and time, is talking to Fenton, the unpleasant boss of a small group of men. The group is in danger and Clara is trying to save them, but Fenton doesn't want to listen to her.

Clara and the Doctor are in Bristol, a city in the south-west of England, where people are disappearing. Are aliens killing them? The Doctor can't help because he can't leave the TARDIS. This time Clara has to be the Doctor. With the help of a young graffiti artist, she tries to understand what is happening. Can she save herself and the men from the aliens? Will the Doctor ever be able to leave the TARDIS? And until he can, will Clara be a good Doctor?

Doctor Who first appeared on television in 1963 in black and white. It was a great success, with its new electronic sounds and crazy stories in outer space. The programmes were shown until 1989. Sixteen years later, *Doctor Who* returned with a new writing team. The stories became funnier and more adult, but the central idea is the same. The Doctor travels through space in the TARDIS, his time machine, fighting aliens. The programmes are shown in many countries around the world.

Peter Capaldi played the Twelfth Doctor. The Doctor always has the same history, but each actor brings something new to the part. Capaldi has always loved *Doctor Who*. When he went into the TARDIS for the first time, he felt at home. 'I know how to work the TARDIS,' he said. 'I've known for a long time!'

Coming Home

A man stood in his sitting-room. He was talking on the phone and he was very frightened.

'Police, please. Hello? Yes. I know who did it. I know who did it all.' His voice was shaking. 'No, no, I *have* to speak quietly. They'll hear me.'

He heard a noise and looked around. The noise got louder.

'Oh, no. Oh, no. Listen. Listen. They're everywhere. All around us. We've been so stupid. *Aargh!*'

Suddenly something pulled him down. He dropped the telephone and went straight into the floor. Only the phone was there, hanging from the wall.

'Hello? Sir?' said the voice on the other end of the phone. 'Are you all right? Are you in trouble? Do you need help? Sir?' But there was no answer.

The man's face was on the wall now. It looked like a strange picture. His eyes were closed but his mouth was open. He was screaming but he made no sound.

Inside the TARDIS, the Doctor stood at the main computer, pressing switches and keys. Clara walked around, putting things into a bag. This was the end of a journey. She wanted to see her boyfriend – Danny – again, back in London. She wanted to be in *her* city, in *her* time.

'You can leave all those things here, you know,' said the Doctor. 'We've got plenty of room – lots and lots of room.' He liked Clara and didn't really want her to go.

'Oh, no. It's all right,' said Clara. 'Danny's a little bit … well, he doesn't want me to keep anything here. But he doesn't mind us travelling together, so that's a little strange. He's happy for me to travel in the TARDIS. So why can't I leave even my toothbrush here? But Danny's not …'

'Sorry,' said the Doctor. 'I stopped listening some time ago.' He was thinking about other things, and looked worried. 'OK. This is the same time that you left. It's also the same place – more or less.'

'More or less?' said Clara. 'What do you mean, "more or less"?'

The Doctor looked at the machine in front of him. 'The computer says "more or less", and that's … strange,' he said.

Clara heard a noise and turned around.

'Er … Doctor, come and see this,' she said.

'Uh-huh?' The Doctor left the computer.

'There's something wrong with the TARDIS door,' she said.

The door wasn't its usual size. It was much smaller. The Doctor went down on his knees to open it. He looked out and, with some difficulty, got through. Clara followed.

From the outside the TARDIS still looked like a police box, but now it was much smaller.

'Well, how did this happen?' the Doctor said. 'We haven't grown. Or have we?' He pulled his sonic screwdriver from his pocket and waved it up and down in front of Clara. 'No – we're the same size,' he said.

Clara looked around. They were on open ground. There were some houses, a wall, a railway line and an old station. She noticed a sign next to the line: BRISTOL.

'Bristol?' she said. 'Doctor, we're in Bristol!'

'Hmm – a hundred and ninety kilometres from London,' said the Doctor.

'Clever.' He looked at the railway and the sign that said BRISTOL. 'We're in the wrong place. That's a problem. But the TARDIS is smaller – that's really, really clever. How has it done that?'

But Clara wanted to be with Danny.

'Yes, I understand – you're excited,' she said impatiently. 'But I live in London. When can I go home?'

'Your house isn't going anywhere,' the Doctor said. 'And mine isn't until I understand this. Can't I just enjoy this for a few minutes? It isn't often that I don't know something.'

Clara stepped towards the door of the TARDIS. She wanted to go back inside but the Doctor stopped her.

'No!' he said. 'I don't think this is dangerous, but …. Well, I don't really know. Also, I need your help. We have to find out how this happened.'

'Fine,' said Clara. 'I'll go and look around.' She walked towards the railway line.

The Doctor pushed himself back through the door into the TARDIS.

The Doctor pushed himself back through the door into the TARDIS.

Rigsy

The shopping centre was quite busy. People walked around from one shop to another. On one side was a big wall, covered with graffiti. Some men were there in green work clothes, each with a number on his jacket. They were painting over the graffiti.

Pots of white paint and paint brushes lay on a table. It had a sign on it which said 'Community Payback*'.

One of them was a young black man. He was painting with a small brush. An older man walked towards him. His name was Fenton and he was the boss. He was not a very nice man.

'It's *your* art – if you can call it that, Rigsy,' Fenton said. 'Let's start with your signature.'

On the wall was Rigsy's name in big blue letters. It was true that the graffiti on the wall was his work.

Fenton picked up a big brush and put it into the white paint. Rigsy was very unhappy but he took the brush. He got down on one knee and started to paint slowly over his signature.

'Faster!' Fenton ordered. 'This is Community Payback, not a holiday.'

---

*Community Payback (or Community Service): work that some criminals can do for their town or city. This means that they don't go to prison.

In the TARDIS the Doctor was trying to find the problem with the computers. He wasn't happy now. Suddenly, the TARDIS moved and the lights flashed. The Doctor almost fell over. He looked around at the lights.

'*I* didn't do that, did I?' he said to himself.

He ran to the door. Then he stopped suddenly, got down and moved his head to one side. The door was even smaller now.

'Oh, this *really* isn't good,' he said.

Clara walked down some steps to an underpass below a road near the shopping centre. At the bottom, there were flowers, toys, cards and photographs on the wall and on the ground, in memory of people who died. Clara stopped and looked at them. She was interested. Who died here and why?

'Don't be sad, love,' a man called.

Clara looked up. It was one of the men from Community Payback. Their work was finished for the morning. They were getting ready to leave. Clara smiled and looked back at the wall.

'Maybe she's lost someone, Stan,' another man, Al, said.

'Oh sorry, love,' said Stan.

'What are they talking about?' Clara thought.

She walked further into the underpass. On the walls were more pictures of people, but the pictures were of their backs not their faces.

Rigsy came down the steps towards her. 'Sorry about them,' he said. He looked back at the men. 'They're stupid.'

'That's all right,' said Clara. 'Don't worry. I've heard worse.'

She smiled. Then she turned back to look at the paintings.

'I've lost someone too,' Rigsy said. 'My aunt Karina. Her hearing wasn't very good.' He walked across and touched the picture of a small woman in a yellow jacket and a black skirt. 'I didn't really know her very well but ... well, she's gone. Have you got a relative here too?'

He walked across and touched the picture of a small woman in a yellow jacket and a black skirt.

'Oh no,' said Clara, 'I haven't lost …'

Rigsy spoke before she finished. 'I'm sure he'll paint her soon.' He smiled. 'I'm not really with those men out there,' he said. 'I just have to do this Community Payback thing.' He looked a little uncomfortable. 'I do graffiti,' he explained. 'Nothing like murder or …'

Clara smiled. 'So what's all this about?' she asked. She looked at the pictures on the walls. 'What's happened to all these people?'

'You mean you don't know?' Rigsy said.

Doctor Oswald

Clara walked back across the open ground at the side of the railway line and phoned the Doctor.

'Hey, I think I've found something,' she said. 'Lots of people are missing around here. Do you think the same thing took them? Is it the thing that's made the TARDIS smaller?'

The Doctor heard her through the loudspeakers on the TARDIS.

'Maybe,' he said.

Clara looked around. She couldn't see the TARDIS anywhere.

'And ... where are *you*?' she asked.

'Exactly where I was,' he replied.

Clara walked around, but she couldn't see the TARDIS anywhere.

'No, you're not. I'm here and I can't see ...'

Then she looked down. The TARDIS was there at her feet, but it was very small now – only about fifteen centimetres high.

'Oh,' she said.

'Yes, oh,' said the Doctor.

She walked around the little TARDIS and laughed.

'That's wonderful,' she said. 'Are you in there?'

'Yes, I am,' the Doctor replied. 'And it's not wonderful. It's very, very serious.'

Inside the TARDIS the Doctor opened a wooden box. He took a small metal device from it, held it up and studied it.

'Are you really small in there?' Clara asked.

She went down on one knee to get closer to the TARDIS.

'No. I'm exactly the same size,' said the Doctor. 'The *outside* size has changed – that's all.'

He walked to the wall. The door was now very small. He opened it and looked out.

From the outside, Clara could only see part of his face. She laughed.

'Stop laughing!' said the Doctor angrily, with his face against the open door. 'This is serious.'

'Yeah, well, I can't help it, can I?' said Clara. 'You and your big old face.' She smiled and shook her head. 'How are you going to get out?'

'Well, I can't. Something is making the TARDIS smaller, and it isn't far away,' he replied.

'Aliens?' asked Clara.

'Maybe. No – what am I saying? *Probably*,' the Doctor said. 'But the TARDIS can't leave now – it's too dangerous. It isn't working well. I don't know what will happen.' He thought for a few seconds. 'Clara, you have to pick up the TARDIS. Carefully. I've changed the weight so you can do it.'

Clara picked it up, very slowly and carefully. She looked through the open door.

'You mean you've made it lighter?' she said.

'Clara, it's *always* lighter,' the Doctor said. 'If the TARDIS ever lands with its *real* weight, it will destroy the Earth.'

He walked carefully back to a computer and looked at the screen.

'Well, maybe that's a story for another time,' Clara said. 'What now?'

'I think I know where the aliens are,' the Doctor said. He went back to the door, pushed his fingers through and pointed. 'They're to the north west. That way.'

The big hand in the small doorway looked strange.

'Please don't do that,' Clara said. 'That's just wrong.'

The Doctor ran back to the controls and picked up two things.

'Now listen,' he said. 'You're going to need these.'

He passed the psychic paper in its holder through the door.

'Oh, wow,' Clara said, taking it in her hand. 'This is wonderful. Does this mean that I'm *you* now?'

'No, it does not,' said the Doctor. He passed out the sonic screwdriver and she took that too. 'So don't get any ideas,' he added.

Clara put the psychic paper, the sonic screwdriver and then the TARDIS in her shoulder bag.

'And put this in your ear,' the Doctor told her.

His hand came out of the bag. He gave her an earphone and she put it in her right ear.

The Doctor ran back to the controls. 'Can you hear me?' he asked.

'Yes,' said Clara, then, feeling a small pain, '*Ow*! What just happened?'

'I've joined the computer to your eyes.'

'What does that mean?' Clara asked.

'I can see what you see,' the Doctor told her.

Back in the shopping centre, Clara turned around. She pointed the screwdriver at some flats, and then at the wall with graffiti on it.

'Can you see anything?' she asked.

'Yes – but nothing useful,' the Doctor said, following her eyes on the computer screen.

Rigsy's face appeared on the screen.

'You never told me your name,' he said to Clara.

'There's no time to make friends,' the Doctor said through the earphone. 'Tell him to go away.'

Clara turned to look at Rigsy. She liked him and wanted to talk to him.

'I'm … er …' She thought for a second, then smiled. 'I'm the Doctor,' she said.

'No, you're not!' the real Doctor said angrily.

'Doctor Oswald,' Clara told Rigsy. She pulled the sonic screwdriver from her bag and pushed a switch. Metal arms came out from the top. 'But you can call me Clara.'

'Doctor Oswald,' Clara told Rigsy. She pulled the sonic screwdriver from her bag and pushed a switch.

They shook hands. 'I'm Rigsy,' he said. 'So ... what are you a doctor *of?*'

'Of lies,' the real Doctor said, from inside the TARDIS.

'Well, I don't really know,' Clara said. 'I just call myself the Doctor.' She smiled. 'I sound important, don't I?'

'Oh, Doctor Oswald, you are so funny,' the Doctor said. 'Could we get back to work, do you think?'

'What *are* you exactly?' Rigsy said. 'I don't think you're police. But that thing –' He pointed to the sonic screwdriver. 'That looks very clever. Are you a spy?'

'Oh, he's a clever one,' the Doctor said. 'Keep him.' But he wasn't serious.

The Empty Flat

The sign outside the flat said *POLICE. DO NOT CROSS*. But Rigsy pushed it to one side and opened the door.

'The owner of this flat was the last person who disappeared,' he said.

It was a small, modern flat with white walls. On a side table there was a cup, a plate and an empty drink can. Perhaps the owner left in a hurry.

On one wall was a strange painting. It looked like an area of very dry earth. It was light brown, and dark lines ran across it. But it wasn't hanging on the wall like a picture. It was painted on the wall.

'When he disappeared, all the doors and windows were locked from the inside,' Rigsy said.

Clara heard the Doctor's voice from the TARDIS: 'Ooh, that's good. I love a good locked room mystery.'

'Yeah, doesn't everyone?' said Clara.

'What?' Rigsy said, because he couldn't hear the Doctor.

Clara turned to face him.

'Huh?' she said, then, 'Oh, sorry. I'm talking to someone.' She pointed to her ear. 'He's listening to our conversation.' She waved her hand at the earphone, then Rigsy, then the earphone again. 'Doctor, this is Rigsy. Rigsy, meet the Doctor,' she said.

'Hello, not very intelligent local person,' the Doctor said from the TARDIS. Rigsy couldn't hear him, of course.

'Another doctor?' he said, with a smile.

This girl was strange, but he liked her.

Clara took the sonic screwdriver from her bag. She pressed a switch and a green light came on. She pointed the screwdriver at a wall and moved it around.

'This is great,' Rigsy said. 'Someone's finally interested. The police weren't doing anything. They *never* do anything around here.'

'Clara,' the Doctor said, 'I don't think we need this boy. He's not very clever. And worse than that, he's wearing a bright yellow jacket.'

'OK, fine,' Clara said impatiently. 'And all those other missing people? Do *you* know where they lived. *He* does.'

Rigsy was looking worried.

'Perhaps he's still in the room.'

Clara turned to look at him.

'Sorry, what?' she said. Rigsy looked a little shy.

'Oh … sorry, nothing,' he said. 'I was just thinking. You know how in some crime stories, a person disappears from inside a locked room? Sometimes they're still *in* the room. But nobody knows they're there.'

Clara didn't answer. She was looking in a mirror on the wall and smiling at the Doctor. He could see her now. So Rigsy wasn't very clever? Really?

'Do you want to go and check another flat?' Rigsy asked.

In the TARDIS, the Doctor moved his face closer to the screen.

'I think that you were wrong about this young man,' he said. 'I think he'll be very useful. He knows the local area.'

'Oh, really?' Clara said. 'I think *I* said that first, not *you*.'

'Never mind, just try not to frighten him away,' the Doctor said.

He didn't understand her feelings at all.

'I'll try very hard,' Clara said.

She was angry now. She pointed the sonic screwdriver at the mirror and turned it on. A green light filled the mirror. Because her eyes saw it, in the TARDIS the Doctor saw it too. The light hurt his eyes and he had to turn his face away from the screen.

Clara started to scan the room again. She checked under the side table.

Rigsy was looking at the painting of dry earth on the wall. 'Maybe he's lost somewhere hot and dry,' he said.

Clara turned to look at the painting. In the TARDIS the Doctor also saw it, on his screen.

'Are we missing something here?' Clara said. 'Missing man, locked room, aliens who can make things small.'

'Sorry,' Rigsy said, 'did you just say say *aliens*?'

Clara turned to face him. She moved close and held up her hand. Her thumb was a few centimetres away from her first finger.

'What if he *is* still in this room, like you said? What if he's here but very small?' she said. 'You know, under the sofa or something.' She ran to the sofa, got down on the floor and looked under it.

The Doctor said, 'Clara, don't frighten him.'

And Rigsy *was* a little frightened.

'OK,' he said, looking at his watch. 'So ... er ... it's nearly the end of my lunch hour. This has been ... interesting.' He moved towards the door.

'Clara!' the Doctor called, 'He's leaving. Do something!'

Clara stood up. 'Rigsy!' she called. 'Wait one second.' She opened her shoulder bag and spoke into it. 'Doctor, open the door of the TARDIS.'

'I didn't mean *that*!' said the Doctor.

'Do you want him to stay or not?' Clara asked him.

She took the TARDIS out of her bag and put it on a shelf.

'Rigsy,' she called. 'Come here. Meet the Doctor.'

Rigsy came back. He looked at the TARDIS. The door was open and the Doctor was standing just inside. Rigsy's mouth fell open.

'Pleased to meet you,' the Doctor said, and waved.

Rigsy looked through the open door of the TARDIS to the room on the other side.

'It's bigger,' he said, 'on the inside.'

The Doctor turned to look around the TARDIS.

'I don't think that's ever been truer,' he agreed.

'What are you?' Rigsy said. 'Aliens, or something?'

Clara was looking at the painting on the wall. She turned around.

'No,' she said. 'Well, *he* is.'

Rigsy smiled. He liked the idea.

An alarm went off inside the TARDIS and the lights flashed. The Doctor looked around the control room. He couldn't understand what was happening.

'Doctor? Doctor, did you hear that?' shouted Clara.

'Yes,' he said. 'Something just took a lot of power from inside the TARDIS.' He looked at the controls.

'*What* did?' Clara asked.

The Doctor ran to the door. The TARDIS was even smaller now.

'I don't know,' he said. 'But that can wait. Just get us out of that flat!' He pushed the door shut.

'OK,' Clara said. She picked up the TARDIS from the shelf and put it under her arm. 'Rigsy,' she said, 'now we run. Stay with me.'

Back in the TARDIS the Doctor was really worried.

'This is terrible,' he said. 'I'm from the people that built the TARDIS. We know about dimensions, so why can't I understand this?'

Clara and Rigsy were walking along the street now.

'Clara,' the Doctor said, 'I need more information. Where have the other people disappeared from?'

In the Walls

Rigsy took Clara into the flat of the first man who disappeared. A policewoman was there. Clara opened the holder with the psychic paper in it and showed it to her.

'MI5*,' she said, introducing herself.

'MI5?' said the policewoman.

She looked at the paper. Her mind said MI5, so the paper also said MI5.

'Yes,' said Clara. 'People are disappearing and we're worried.'

'Well, you've come to the right place,' the policewoman said. 'This was the first reported disappearance, a Mr Heath.'

She gave the holder back. Clara waved it in front of Rigsy's face. She was proud of what it could do. Rigsy looked at it and smiled.

'It's not near the others,' the policewoman continued, 'but it happened in exactly the same way.'

In the TARDIS, the Doctor was excited. He was running around, looking for something.

'Clara,' he said, 'I think your idea about very small people was wrong.'

Clara could feel the TARDIS move as the Doctor ran around. She put a hand to her earphone.

*MI5: British secret police

'Doctor, what are you doing?' she asked.

The policewoman was still looking around the room.

'They just disappeared,' she said.

'An idea has just come to me,' the Doctor said. 'Locked room mysteries. The first possibility is that they're still in the room. The second is that they're in the walls.'

He ran to the door of the TARDIS with a big hammer in his hand.

'What do you mean, they're in the ...' Clara said, then she felt something move in her bag.

She put her hand in and slowly pulled out the hammer. It came out through the door of the TARDIS.

The policewoman was talking with her back to them but Clara wasn't listening.

'It seems that they're in the walls,' she said.

The policewoman turned around and looked at the hammer.

Rigsy took it and hit one of the walls hard. Pieces fell out. He gave the hammer to Clara.

The policewoman's phone rang.

'PC* Forrest,' she said, walking away. 'Yes, sir. They're from MI5, sir.' She left the room.

Clara hit the wall. More pieces fell.

'So,' said Rigsy, 'you and that man in a box. Do you do this sort of thing a lot?

'Oh, well, he's usually out of the box,' Clara said, 'but yes.' She hit the wall again.

In Mr Heath's sitting-room, PC Forrest was still talking to her boss. 'I don't know why they're here.' She closed the door. 'Maybe they thought we weren't doing enough, sir,' she said, as Rigsy and Clara continued to hit the wall.

Suddenly, behind PC Forrest, there was a strange sound. The wall began to move like water and she turned and looked at it.

'Wait a second,' she said quickly.

She switched on her torch and looked closely at the wall.

*PC: the title of a police officer

'Sir,' she said on her phone, 'there's something in here, I think.'

In the other room Clara was still using the hammer.

'So how did you get this job?' Rigsy asked. 'Did you study science, or aliens, or something?'

Clara laughed. 'No,' she said. 'It's more of a right place right time thing. Or wrong place wrong time if he's not being nice.'

She hit the wall again, hard.

In the TARDIS the Doctor said, 'I *can* hear you, you know.'

PC Forrest was still shining her torch at the sitting-room walls. But the floor was moving like water now too. It was moving towards her feet.

'Sir,' she said on her phone, 'there's something in here, I think.'

She was suddenly very frightened.

She looked down. Then she screamed as her leg was pulled down into the floor. She dropped the torch. Then she fought unsuccessfully to get free.

Clara and Rigsy ran towards the sitting-room.

Still screaming, PC Forrest was pulled into the floor. First her body, then her face disappeared.

Clara pushed the door open.

'PC Forrest!' she shouted.

The torch, still on, was lying on the floor. There was nothing unusual about the room, but there was nobody there.

Clara looked at Rigsy. Then she walked to the torch and picked it up.

'Doctor, she's gone,' she said.

Everything was quiet in the room now. They looked around. There was a large painting on the wall and some modern furniture. In the centre of the room a chair hung from the ceiling. It was shaped like a ball.

In the TARDIS the Doctor was walking up and down, thinking.

'What am I missing?' he said. 'The TARDIS can understand everything in the known universe.' An idea suddenly came to him, and he stopped walking. 'The *known* universe. Maybe that's the answer!'

Clara looked at the painting. It was orange, and red lines were painted on it. Was that the shape of a tree?

'*This* universe!' the Doctor said.

On the computer screen he could see what Clara saw.

Her eyes moved past the painting.

'Clara, wait, go back,' he said. 'Back, back, back. That painting.'

Clara turned to look at it again.

'That's a map of how blood moves around the body,' the Doctor said. 'But it's bigger and flat.'

Clara pointed the sonic screwdriver at the painting.

'I think we've found PC Forrest,' the Doctor said. 'Well, what's left of her.'

'That shows how her blood moves – moved?' Clara asked.

The Doctor walked to his computer. He touched the screen and brought back some earlier pictures from the scanner.

'The painting in the other flat,' he said. 'That wasn't dry earth at all. It was a large picture of a small piece of someone's skin.'

'What?' said Clara. 'Why?'

'I don't know who or what the aliens are,' the Doctor said. 'But they're testing us. They're – they're cutting us up. They're trying to understand us.' He thought for a few seconds. 'Yes! They're trying to understand three dimensions.'

Just then they heard the soft sound of the door shutting. Rigsy reached for the handle, then pulled his hand back.

'*Ow*! The handle's hot,' he said.

'Doctor,' Clara said. 'The handle – they've flattened it.'

And it *was* flat, like a picture of a handle. The Doctor saw it on his screen. 'Interesting,' he said – then, more urgently, 'Clara, they're in the walls!'

Clara and Rigsy looked around. The walls were moving.

'Keep away from them,' the Doctor said. 'If they touch you, you're finished.'

The sofa went flat and lay on the floor like a picture. The Doctor watched on his screen. He was shaking his head and trying to understand.

'What will happen if they touch us?' Rigsy said.

An armchair went flat.

'I really don't want to find out,' Clara said.

They moved to the centre of the room. Rigsy looked at the round chair hanging from the ceiling. He jumped into it and Clara followed him. She stood up in the chair.

'They can't jump, can they?' Rigsy asked.

Then Clara's phone rang. She took it out of her bag and looked at the screen. Oh, no! It was her boyfriend. This was not the best time for a phone call. She shook her head and thought for a few seconds, then answered it.

'Hey, you,' she said, smiling.

'I'm on our seat in the park,' Danny said. 'Are you going to be *very* late?'

'They can't jump, can they?' Rigsy asked.

He couldn't understand why she wasn't there.

'Just a little,' Clara said. She looked at the floor. It was moving now, closer and closer to the centre of the room. 'Sorry, Danny,' she said. 'I don't think I can be there for lunch.'

'But it's so nice in the park,' Danny said.

From the TARDIS the Doctor said, 'Clara, the window!'

'Look! Look!' Rigsy shouted. 'They're climbing the walls!'

The walls were moving in waves, higher and higher. The aliens were trying to get to the chair.

Danny heard Rigsy's voice.

'Who was that?' he asked.

'Er ... that's just a man on Community Payback. I'm helping him find his aunt,' Clara said.

In the TARDIS the Doctor heard her.

'Nice,' he said. 'Not really lying.'

Clara and Rigsy were making the chair move from one side to the other. They were trying to get closer to the window. Clara cried out.

'Is something happening?' Danny asked.

He clearly didn't understand why she was with another man, and not in the park with him.

'Er ... yeah, there was a thing, er ... a thing,' Clara said, as they moved the chair more and more.

'Where are you and are you in trouble?' Danny said calmly.

Clara looked up. They didn't have much time left.

'No, no, no, I'm fine!' she called.

She took out the sonic screwdriver and pointed it at the window. It pulled the chair free of the ceiling and out of the flat.

'*Aargh*!' Rigsy screamed.

Danny heard the crash and Rigsy's scream.

'Clara? Clara?' he called, very worried now.

Still inside the chair, Clara and Rigsy landed in the garden.

Your Only Hope

Clara fought to get out of the chair.

'Danny?' she said into her phone.

'What's happening?' Danny said urgently.

'Oh, not much,' Clara answered as she stood up. 'It's a long story.'

Now Rigsy, too, was able to stand up.

'*What* story?' Danny said.

'I'll tell you later,' Clara said. They ran out of the garden and into the street. 'I love you.'

In the TARDIS the Doctor was excited now.

'This explains everything,' he said. 'These aliens are from a universe with only two dimensions – and yes, that *is* interesting! People have believed in a universe like that for a long time. But nobody could go there and prove it. Well, not without losing a lot of weight.'

He looked up and spoke to Clara. 'And what long story are you going to tell Danny? Or haven't you made it up yet?'

Clara and Rigsy were walking back towards the underpass.

'Sorry, what?' she said. 'What was that?'

'That was excellent lying, Doctor Oswald,' the Doctor said.

'Yeah? Well, I thought it was quite weak myself,' Clara said unhappily.

'I meant to *me*,' the Doctor said. 'Danny's OK about you being back in the TARDIS? Didn't you tell me that?'

'Well … he is,' Clara said.

'Yeah, because he doesn't know anything about it,' said the Doctor.

'Uh … Well, no …' she agreed. 'But …'

'Well done,' the Doctor said. 'Lying is an important skill.'

'Well, that's good,' she said, but she still looked unhappy.

'And not very nice,' the Doctor added.

Clara could hear strange noises in her ear. She stopped walking and put her hand to the earphone.

'Doctor, I can't hear you as well,' she said.

'What?' the Doctor said. He ran to the computer and looked at the screen. 'Oh, maybe something happened to the earphone when you went through the window. Take it out and use the sonic screwdriver.'

'I'm doing it,' Clara said, pulling the earphone from her ear.

Rigsy walked around the corner to the underpass. The men were holding tins of paint and brushes. They were ready to paint over the pictures of people on the walls.

'Hey! They can't do that. Hey! What are you doing?' he shouted to the boss.

'We're doing our job,' Fenton said. 'And I'm going to report you. You're late back from lunch.'

On the steps of the underpass, Clara had the earphone in one hand and the sonic screwdriver in the other. She hated the idea of lying to Danny.

'Is it still lying if you're doing it for the good of the listener?' she said.

She held the screwdriver up to the earphone. Then she switched the screwdriver on for a few seconds to mend the earphone.

She was looking inside the underpass as Rigsy said angrily, 'You can't paint over these pictures! They're of the people who died. They're memories.'

'They're graffiti. The city doesn't want them here,' Fenton said. 'Stan!' he ordered. 'Start covering them.'

Stan walked towards a wall. In his hand was a big brush covered in white paint. Rigsy moved towards him and took the brush from Stan's hand.

Clara walked into the underpass. Now the Doctor could see Rigsy and the men.

'Clara! Talk to me, talk to me!' he said.

But Clara still had the earphone in her hand and couldn't hear him.

The Doctor ran to the door of the TARDIS and pushed his hand out. It came out of Clara's shoulder bag and she felt it touch her arm.

'Clara, the paintings. It's the paintings!' he shouted, and she heard him from inside her bag. Then his finger pointed. 'Over there, look, the paintings! We've found the missing people. They're *in the walls*!'

Clara looked at the walls and put her earphone back in.

'What do I do?' she asked.

'Stay calm, but get everyone out,' the Doctor told her.

Clara walked into the group of men.

'They're very good,' she said. 'Who painted them?'

'I don't know. A local artist,' Rigsy said. 'Probably someone in the family of one of them.'

'Did you ever *meet* the artist?' Clara asked. 'Or did the pictures just appear after people disappeared?'

'And who are you, love?' Fenton asked angrily.

Clara took out the holder with the psychic paper. She opened it and showed it to Fenton.

'Health and Safety,' she said. 'This underpass is unsafe. Everyone needs to leave immediately.'

Fenton looked at the psychic paper and gave it back.

'There's nothing on it,' he said. 'Try again, love.'

Clara was surprised and the Doctor was too.

'What?' he said. 'You can only see *nothing* on psychic paper if you have no imagination at all.'

'Stan, do your job,' Fenton said.

Stan moved towards the wall.

'Clara, stop him!' said the Doctor, but it was too late.

When Stan's brush touched the wall, he was pulled into it.

'Stan!' shouted Rigsy, but Stan was gone.

Then the pictures on the wall started to move. Slowly, they turned around to face into the underpass.

'What is this? What are they?' one of the men, Al, shouted.

'The aliens are hiding in the dead,' the Doctor said. 'They're *wearing* them.'

'Forget Stan. Your friend's gone,' Clara said.

Like all the others, she was frightened.

'Clara, get them out of there!' the Doctor shouted.

'We need to move. Now!' Clara said.

The men all turned and ran away. The pictures moved down from the walls and onto the ground, then began to follow them.

The Doctor watched as Clara and the others ran into an old railway building. Clara was last and closed the door behind her. They walked quickly along the side of some old trains.

One of the men, George, said, 'Did they follow us? I didn't see them follow us. Are we safe?'

'Are we really hiding from killer graffiti?' Al said. 'This is crazy.'

In the TARDIS the Doctor heard him.

'I agree,' he said. 'We'll have to think of a better name for them than that.'

'And Stan was one of them,' George said. 'Flattened, dead, but coming after us.'

'Clara, this is an important time,' the Doctor said. 'These men are frightened. They don't know what's happening. But soon they'll want to follow someone. You need to make sure that they follow *you*.'

Clara was behind the group because she was scanning with the sonic screwdriver.

'OK, I'll do it,' she said. She walked more quickly. 'George,' she called out. 'You're George, aren't you? Can you watch that area?' She pointed across one of the railway lines. 'If anything moves, shout, OK?'

Fenton stepped nearer and faced her.

'He won't do anything until I get some answers,' he said. 'Who are you? That's what I want to know.' Clara walked past him and the others to the front. Fenton continued, 'You say that you're from the government. I don't believe you. And this is a railway building. You shouldn't be here.'

Clara turned to face him.

'Seriously?' she said.

'Seriously,' said Fenton.

'Fine, I'll tell you who I am,' Clara said. She moved closer to him and spoke quietly into his ear. 'I'm your only hope of staying alive. That's who I am.'

7

Into the Tunnel

Clara continued walking. Then she stopped in front of a wall and turned.

'Rigsy,' she said, 'how well do you know this area?' She pointed to a door. 'Do you know what's on the other side of that door?'

'It's the old Brunswick line,' Rigsy said. 'But it's not safe.'

'Well, it's not *too* dangerous,' Al said.

'I know it,' Rigsy said. 'I've been down here a few times.'

'Yeah,' Fenton said. 'I'm sure you've spent a lot of time down here. You were probably painting things on the walls.'

'Yeah, well, maybe you'll be glad that he did,' Clara said. 'If those things come in here, that's our only way out.' She walked away from the group and said quietly to the Doctor, 'I hope I can keep them all alive.'

'Ah, welcome to my world,' the Doctor said. 'So what's next, Doctor Clara?'

'Lie to them,' said Clara.

'What?' the Doctor said.

'Lie to them. Give them hope. Tell them that they're all going to be fine,' Clara said. 'Isn't that what *you* do?'

'Sometimes,' he said. 'People with hope usually run faster. Without that hope, they'll ...'

'Run more slowly and die,' said Clara.

Fenton and Al were listening. 'Who's she talking to?' Fenton asked.

'Rigsy says she's from MI5,' Al said.

'Right, now maybe this will help you,' the Doctor said. 'Do you remember the graffiti from the underpass? In places, it looked like footsteps on the walls.'

'I remember,' Clara said.

'Well, I don't think it *was* graffiti,' the Doctor said. 'That's how those aliens saw us. It's how we look in two-dimensional space. They were trying to talk to us, but we couldn't hear them. Then they moved on to flattening and cutting up. They were trying to understand, trying to be like us.' He pointed his finger at the screen. 'But here's the big question,' he continued. 'Do they know they're hurting us?'

'You think this is all one big mistake?' Clara asked.

'That's a very good question,' the Doctor replied. 'Why don't we ask them?' Then he explained how. 'Rigsy,' Clara said. 'There's a ladder over there. Can you get it?'

Above the platform there were loudspeakers. Rigsy brought the ladder and put it under them. Clara climbed the ladder and held the sonic screwdriver up to the loudspeakers.

'We need a way to talk to them,' the Doctor said.

They could all hear him because his voice went from the screwdriver to the loudspeakers. The Doctor ran through the TARDIS, looking for something.

'Why can't the TARDIS turn their language into English?' Clara asked.

'Because their idea of language is as strange as their idea of space,' the Doctor said. He had the tool that he wanted. He ran back to the computer. 'Even the TARDIS doesn't understand them.'

From under the ladder Fenton said, 'This is a bad idea. Why does your friend think that the aliens want to talk?'

'Out in space,' the Doctor said, 'I know some living things that are made of intelligent gas. They throw balls of fire as a friendly wave. I know other aliens with sixty-four stomachs. They talk by cutting one open.'

'He's got an idea,' Clara told the men.

'The universe is very big and very strange. You can't be so quick to judge,' said the Doctor. He found a small silver box and ran back to the controls. 'Perhaps these aliens don't even understand that we *need* three dimensions.' He got down, reached under the controls and with some difficulty fitted the box. 'Perhaps they don't even know that they're hurting us.'

Clara thought about this. It didn't seem possible.

'Do you really believe that?' she asked.

'No. But I really hope that I'm right. I *want* to be right. We don't want to fight with friendly aliens.' The Doctor started to type on the computer. 'Let's start with some numbers. Even in a flat world they'll have numbers.'

As he typed, the light on the screwdriver flashed. Strange sounds came out of the loudspeakers.

'They're answering,' the Doctor said. 'The TARDIS is working on their language now.'

Clara and the men waited.

'It's a number,' the Doctor said. 'They're giving us a number – 55.'

'55?' said Clara. 'What does that mean?'

'I know what it means,' Rigsy said. 'We all have numbers on our jackets.' He showed that he had the number 52 on his jacket, just above the pocket. 'That was the number on Stan's jacket – the man they killed in the underpass.'

'They're laughing at us,' Fenton said, always quick to think badly of someone.

'We don't know that,' said the Doctor.

'Perhaps they're saying sorry,' Clara said.

'Really?' said Al. 'That's nice of them.' He didn't mean it.

'Saying *sorry*? Are you seriously …?' Fenton began, but more sounds came from the loudspeakers.

'Be quiet. Listen. Wait,' Clara told him. She put her hand to her earphone.

'Two two,' said the Doctor. '22.'

'22,' Clara repeated.

Each man looked at the others.

'That's George,' said Rigsy.

They all turned to look at George. He touched the number 22 on his jacket and looked very frightened.

'It's your turn next, George,' said Fenton. He turned to Clara, and added angrily, 'Now they're trying to start a fight.'

'Maybe,' said Clara. 'Or maybe they're showing us that they can read.'

'Oh, grow up,' Fenton said impatiently. 'They're choosing the next one to die.'

Clara stepped towards George. He wasn't moving.

'George?' she said.

From the TARDIS the Doctor said, 'Clara, be careful.'

She saw that George was now just two-dimensional. Then his shape broke down and he disappeared into the wall and the floor. The others watched in fear.

'Quick!' said Clara. 'The tunnel.'

They ran into it.

Two Dimensions or Three?

They stopped some way inside the tunnel and the men sat down. They didn't know what to do.

'Doctor, they've got George,' Clara said.

'I know,' said the Doctor. 'I saw it happen.'

'What now?' asked Clara.

'Give me a minute. I'm working on it,' the Doctor said. He was at his work table. There were plans open and there were some numbers on a piece of paper. He was making something.

Clara walked a little way along the tunnel and looked around. There was no railway line because the tunnel wasn't in use anymore. She shone her torch on a door. The handle was a big metal wheel, but it was as flat as a picture.

'Another flat handle,' she said. 'They were here.' She shone her torch around. 'But they're not here now,' she said. She turned and walked back towards the others. 'They've stopped following us, I think,' she said to the Doctor. 'Maybe they're pushing us into a corner.'

'You're thinking like someone from Earth,' the Doctor said. 'These aliens come from another dimension.'

'That's three exits, all closed by them,' Al said, when she returned to the group.

Clara walked past him and spoke to Rigsy. 'Where's the next exit?' she asked.

'I can only think of one more,' Rigsy said. 'It's where the old line joins the new one. But it's a long walk. It's quicker through that door.'

Fenton was sitting on a box. He looked up.

'But we can't get through it, can we?' he said angrily.

'I'm just saying,' said Rigsy.

'Clara,' the Doctor said, 'maybe I can help with that door.' He was at his work table, putting something together. 'Give me five minutes,' he told her. Clara and the men walked along the tunnel. Rigsy was at the front. They shone their torches on the walls as they walked.

Rigsy stopped. On the wall in front of him was a painting. It was taller than he was. It went most of the way across the tunnel. He smiled.

'It's one of mine. Do you like it?' he asked.

Clara looked at it quickly.

'Yeah, not bad,' she said, and she continued walking. Rigsy looked sad. It was important to him that she liked his work.

'So, what's this thing that you're working on?' she said to the Doctor.

'I've found a way to bring things back to three dimensions,' the Doctor said. 'I think it'll work for smaller things, like door handles.'

'It's one of mine. Do you like it?' he asked.

'So, what is it?' Clara said. 'A de-flattener?'

'We're *not* calling it a de-flattener!' the Doctor said.

He ran to the door of the TARDIS and pushed his hand out. His hand came out of Clara's bag and he gave the device to her. It looked like an old phone with some other pieces added to it.

'It's called the 2Dis – two dimensions!' He laughed. 'Try it!' he told her.

Clara went back to the door and the others followed. She pointed the device at the flat wheel that was the door handle. Circles of green light shone from the device and moved towards the handle, but it didn't change. The device began to shake. It grew hotter and smoke came out of it. Then there was a loud noise like an electrical failure and the 2Dis died.

Clara put it into her bag and gave it back to the Doctor. She looked at the others and smiled sadly.

'We'll take the longer way,' she said.

They moved away, down the tunnel.

On the TARDIS, lights started to flash and an alarm went off. The Doctor looked around, then pressed keys on the controls.

'Clara, I don't know how, but they're doing it again,' the Doctor said. 'They're stealing energy from the TARDIS.'

Clara stopped walking. 'How?' she asked. 'Your door's closed.'

'It's different this time,' the Doctor said.

Clara ran after the men. 'Listen!' she said. 'The Doctor thinks we're in trouble. He thinks they're close.'

Fenton looked at her. 'Where, exactly?' he asked.

'I don't know. He's not sure,' said Clara. 'He's getting signs of them all around us.'

Something made a shadow in the light coming down the tunnel.

'Oh, that's great,' Fenton said. 'It sounds important but means nothing. Can you tell your friend ...?'

A very large hand moved quickly and silently down the tunnel. It lifted Al into the air and took him away.

'*Aargh!*' Al screamed, as it pulled him away from them towards a strong white light.

The Doctor saw it all on the screen in the TARDIS.

'Of course,' he said. 'This is the next stage. The aliens are becoming three-dimensional.'

From all over the tunnel floor, dark shapes began to appear. First there were hands, then arms. Then they grew bigger and bigger, and complete bodies climbed out. They had the faces of PC Forrest, George, Al, Stan and the other dead people.

'Run!' shouted Rigsy.

The group turned and ran back down the tunnel.

Clara stopped at the door.

'Doctor?' she said. 'The door. Can you help with the handle?'

The Doctor passed the 2Dis to her, out of her bag.

'I've made it stronger,' he said.

'And it will work this time?' Clara asked.

'Oh yes,' the Doctor said.

Clara pointed the 2Dis at the door and switched it on. This time it worked. The wheel on the door quickly became three-dimensional again. Rigsy turned it and opened the door, then they all ran through. On the other side, he turned the wheel again to lock the door. Then they began to run.

'Clara, stop!' the Doctor said. 'Use the 2Dis again! It will make the handle two-dimensional again.'

'There's a ladder at the end of this tunnel,' Rigsy said. 'If we go down into the tunnel below, we can climb out into daylight.'

'Wait! Wait!' Clara said.

She pointed the 2Dis at the wheel on the door and switched it on. It changed the handle into two dimensions.

'If it's flat, are we safe now?' Fenton asked.

'They can't get through, can they?' asked Rigsy.

On the other side of the door, the shadowy shapes moved towards it. Energy came from their hands and hit the door. The wheel became three-dimensional again.

The group ran away, down the tunnel.

The Doctor watched on the screen.

'This is new,' he said to himself. 'Now that they're three-dimensional, they can change two dimensions into three.'

Clara pointed the 2Dis at the door and switched it on.

The door opened and two shapes like Stan and PC Forrest came through, followed by George and Al.

'Clara,' the Doctor said, 'do you want the good news or the bad news?'

'We're *in* the bad news!' Clara shouted as she ran. 'I'm *living* the bad news!'

'This is the good news. I know how to send them back to their own dimension,' the Doctor said.

'Do it! Now!' Clara shouted.

The group was still running and the shapes were following them.

'And that's the bad news,' the Doctor said. 'I can't do it *now*. The TARDIS hasn't got enough power. It won't work.'

'Great!' shouted Clara. 'What do you want me to do about it?'

'Well, I'm sure these aliens can push energy out as fast as they can steal it,' the Doctor said.

Clara stopped running.

'Maybe if I ask them really nicely, they'll give some energy back to the TARDIS,' she said, unamused.

Suddenly Fenton shouted, 'I've had enough!' He pulled the TARDIS out of Clara's bag. 'Give me that machine!' he said.

Rigsy tried to take the TARDIS back from him, but it flew out of Fenton's hands and fell down a deep, dark hole!

Clara watched it fall.

'Doctor!' she shouted.

No Way In, No Way Out

The TARDIS hit the ground at the bottom of the hole. Inside, the Doctor was badly shaken. The lights went off and on and alarms sounded. The Doctor looked up. He was frightened.

Clara looked down into the hole and put her hand over the earphone. 'Hello? Doctor?' she shouted.

There was no reply.

Fenton and Rigsy were ready to fight. Clara stepped between them.

'Can you please do this later?' she said. 'We need to move.'

She left them. The shapes were still coming down the tunnel, getting closer and closer.

In the TARDIS the Doctor hit the controls with his hand, again and again. Nothing happened.

'Doctor?' Clara said urgently through the earphone. 'Doctor, I dropped you down a hole. Where are you?'

He looked up.

'I don't know,' he said. He ran around and hit some other controls. 'Nothing's working,' he said. 'Another fall like that and I'm finished.'

The TARDIS was lying on its side. The Doctor opened the door, then turned his head. Now he could look out with both eyes.

'Er ... I'm on a train line,' he said. He could see a light far away, along the tunnel. 'And there's a train coming.'

He was thinking of ways to move the TARDIS. But each one needed power.

'Can't *you* move the TARDIS?' Clara asked urgently.

'Clara, there's no power,' the Doctor said. 'The TARDIS can't boil an egg now. Listen, do what you can. Get those people out of there. You're stronger than you know.'

Rigsy came to Clara and looked down.

'I hope they can't climb down ladders,' he said.

She didn't answer him.

'No,' she said to the Doctor. 'I mean – *you* move the TARDIS. Push your hand out and use your fingers.'

'What a good idea!' the Doctor thought.

He ran to the door. He pushed his hand out and stood the TARDIS up. Then he walked his fingers and pulled the TARDIS behind him. He reached the side of the line and pulled the TARDIS over it successfully. He stood up and walked back from the door.

'Ah!' he said happily.

He danced a few steps.

But then the ground shook with the movement of the train and the TARDIS fell over. Inside it, the Doctor almost fell too.

He went back to the door and looked out. He could see that the top of the TARDIS was on the line again. Now the train was very close. He threw himself onto the floor and under the controls. Then he reached up and pulled a switch.

Clara listened to her earphone. There was silence.

'Doctor?' she said, worried. 'Doctor?'

Rigsy and Fenton climbed down the ladder to the railway line. They both had torches.

'They aren't here,' Rigsy said. 'Where are they?'

'There's no other way down, right?' Fenton asked. Rigsy turned away and didn't answer. 'Hey! I'm talking to you,' Fenton said.

'There is,' said Rigsy. 'There's an old lift near the mouth of the tunnel.'

Clara was climbing down the ladder.

'We should go,' she said, as she reached the bottom.

Fenton looked along the tunnel.

'Oh no,' he said. There were moving shadows against the light at the end. The aliens! They heard a noise and turned. 'And there's a train coming on this line too,' Fenton said.

There was no way out. The aliens were at one end of the tunnel and a train was speeding towards them from the other end. What could they do?

The train was moving fast. A sign at the front said, 'Not in use'.

Clara pulled out the sonic screwdriver. She pointed it at the light at the side of the line and changed it from green to red. The train driver saw it. The wheels screamed as the train came to a stop.

Inside the TARDIS the Doctor pulled his coat more tightly around him.

'I don't know if you can still hear me out there,' he said. 'The TARDIS has now completely shut down. No way in, no way out. I was able to turn it off just before the train hit. That protected it. But there's not enough power left now to start it again.'

Bill, the driver, climbed down his ladder from the train.

'What's happening?' he asked. 'Why the red light?'

Clara pulled out the holder with the psychic paper in it and showed it to him.

'MI5,' she said. 'We've got a ... er ...' She couldn't think of a reason for stopping the train.

'There's something along there in the tunnel,' Fenton said. 'Nothing can get through until we've cleared it.'

For a stupid person, this was a good idea.

Bill looked at the psychic paper. He believed that Clara was from MI5.

Rigsy turned and ran back along the train.

'Can we drive your train into it?' Clara asked the driver. 'The train's empty, isn't it?'

She looked along the tunnel. The shadows of the aliens were coming closer.

'Yeah, it's out of use,' Bill said, 'but someone has to hold the dead man's handle or it won't move.'

'Dead man's handle?' Clara asked.

'You have to hold it when you're driving,' Bill said. 'If you take your hand off it, the train stops. So if a driver dies when ...'

'Yes, yes, I understand,' Clara said.

'Is this really for MI5?' Bill said, smiling. 'I've always wanted to drive a train into something.'

'Sorry – we have to send the train in without a driver,' Clara told him.

Suddenly, the train began to move. Clara ran and climbed onto it. She got through a door some way back from the front and pulled it shut behind her.

'Rigsy!' she shouted.

She ran through the train as it went faster and faster. Then she reached the front and stopped. Rigsy was sitting at the controls.

'What are you doing?' she said quietly.

'I'm going to drive into the aliens,' Rigsy said. 'It'll give you some time to get away.'

'You'll die,' Clara said.

'Yeah, of course I'll die,' Rigsy said. 'Now go!'

'Is this really for MI5?' Bill said, smiling. 'I've always wanted to drive a train into something.'

'Well, why do you want to die?'

'Just go, OK?' Rigsy said.

'OK, fine, yeah,' Clara said. 'And I'll always remember you.'

She put her hand into her bag. 'Fine. Great,' said Rigsy.

'But I'm just going to do this.'

She took a hairband from her bag and put it around the dead man's handle. Then she tied the other end lower down. Now the handle couldn't move and the train couldn't stop.

'It doesn't need a driver now,' she said. She moved back and stood at the door. 'And I really like that hairband. So shall I take it off again? And in the future, shall I remember the brave man who died for it?'

Rigsy shook his head. He didn't know what to do.

'Let's go,' Clara said. 'You're not going to get away from me so easily. There's work to do.'

Rigsy looked through the driver's window one more time. He wanted to drive the train and save the others. But he knew that Clara was right. He stood up. Clara took his hand and pulled and they ran back through the train. Clara opened an outside door and they jumped out. They hit the ground hard at the side of the line.

The noise of the train stopped as they sat up. They looked along the tunnel. The train wasn't a train now. It was a two-dimensional picture along one side of the tunnel.

'I really did like that hairband,' Clara said.

Shapes began to grow out of the tunnel floor.

'It didn't work!' Clara shouted.

She and Rigsy stood up and started to run back down the tunnel. Suddenly, Clara saw something at her feet. She stopped and picked it up. It was a square blue box with circles and lines on each side.

'What is it?' asked Rigsy.

Clara turned it around in her hands and looked at it.

'I think it's the TARDIS,' she said.

Rigsy looked back. More shapes were coming out of the tunnel floor. The aliens stood up and started to move.

Clara held tightly on to the TARDIS as she and Rigsy ran.

Rigsy's Painting

Clara, Rigsy, Fenton and Bill ran inside a building and found an office. The office was old and dirty. Nobody used it now. There were old railway posters, photographs and maps on the walls. A book, some envelopes and papers lay on a long table in the centre of the room. Other books lay on desks and shelves.

Clara turned away from the others, walked across the room and looked closely at the TARDIS. She pressed her earphone more tightly into her ear, trying to hear the Doctor.

'Doctor?' she called urgently.

Behind her, Fenton and Rigsy told the train driver about the aliens.

'They wear your skin?' Bill asked.

'They do now,' Fenton said. 'I preferred them when they were flat.'

'This is crazy,' Bill said.

'Doctor?' Clara said again. There was no answer. 'Doctor? What can I do now?' She turned the box around. 'No – what *shall* I do now?'

She knew that she had to make her own decisions.

She walked over to the table, holding up the box.

'OK, OK … OK,' she said, thinking. The three men stood around the table and looked at her. 'The TARDIS needs energy,' she said. 'If it has power, the Doctor can save us.'

She looked around the room. On the desk there were some old railway posters. She looked at Rigsy. He was still carrying his bag with tins of paint in it. Clara had an idea. She smiled and picked up one of the posters.

She put it flat on the table and turned it over. Then she took a tin of paint from Rigsy's bag and shook it.

'Leave her,' Fenton said. 'She's gone crazy.'

He turned and walked to the door, but he didn't leave the room.

'Are you OK?' Rigsy asked Clara.

'Yeah, are you?' Clara said.

She was smiling as she shook the can.

'I think I *will* be,' said Rigsy. He clearly believed in Clara. 'What's this?'

'Now, Graffiti Boy,' Clara said, 'I've got a job for you.'

She threw him the tin.

Rigsy caught it.

'I'm always happy to paint,' he said. 'But I don't think this is the best time.'

'Well, OK, if you don't think you can do it,' Clara said.

Rigsy thought for a few seconds. Then he threw the tin in the air and caught it. He put it down on the table. Then he put his hands there, looking at the paper.

'What do you need, exactly?' he asked.

Clara walked along the tunnel with a torch in one hand and the TARDIS in the other. She found a place for the TARDIS on a narrow shelf. Then she, Rigsy, Fenton and Bill climbed the ladder up to the first tunnel.

'We're all going to die. This plan's crazy,' Fenton said.

'You want to walk away? Walk. You want to stay? Then be quiet!' said Clara.

'They're coming!' Bill cried.

There were six of them. They looked similar to PC Forrest and Stan and the other dead people, but they were more like moving pictures. The aliens walked slowly, moving from side to side. Then they came to a door in the wall at the side of the tunnel. The round handle on the door was flat.

In the TARDIS the lights were low. It was still losing power and the Doctor was only able to move slowly and with difficulty.

'There isn't much more air and it's getting colder,' he said. 'I don't know if you'll ever hear this, Clara.' He looked very tired. 'I don't even know if you're still alive out there,' he continued.

Clara *could* hear him. She listened and felt very sad.

The aliens stood in front of the door. They held up their arms and rivers of energy flew through the air towards the handle. It was exactly as Clara thought. They were trying to make it three-dimensional again.

'But you were good!' the Doctor said loudly. Then he added, more quietly, 'And you made a very fine Doctor.'

His eyes closed and his head went down.

The aliens poured more and more energy into the door. Clara, Rigsy, Fenton and Bill watched.

The aliens stood in front of the door They held up their arms and rivers of energy flew through the air towards the handle.

'It's not working,' Fenton said angrily. 'You've killed us all.'

'Is this going to save us?' Bill asked. 'You're just putting energy into the door.'

Clara shook her head. 'No,' she said. 'Not *into* the door. *Through* the door. When your enemies are strong, you have to use that against them.'

The door wasn't, in fact, a door. It was a very good *painting* of a door, by Rigsy, on the back of the railway poster. When he finished it, Clara put it on the wall. Then on the other side of the wall she placed the little blue box – the TARDIS. Now the energy was passing through the wall and into the TARDIS.

'They can't make the door three-dimensional because it never *was* three-dimensional,' Clara told the others. 'They don't know that it's just a picture.'

The poster was hot now and it started to fall off the wall. But on the other side of the wall, the TARDIS began to shake. Inside, the lights came on again. The Doctor moved his head up, then back, and took in some air. Power! He ran down the steps to the controls and started to press switches.

The TARDIS shot up into the air. It turned round and round and became larger. Suddenly, it flew past the aliens and away down the tunnel. Clara smiled. Then the TARDIS flew back again. It was full size! It landed hard in front of the aliens, sent out a green field of light and pushed the aliens back.

'The plan worked,' Clara said, laughing.

From inside the TARDIS, the Doctor spoke to the aliens. His voice, through the loudspeakers, was very serious.

'I tried to talk to you. I want you to remember that,' he told them. 'I tried to understand you. But I think that you understand *us* perfectly now. And I think that you just aren't interested.'

He didn't want to kill them. In fact, he didn't even want to send them away. They were strange and different and interesting. He wanted to learn from them. But *they* only wanted to learn how to *destroy* people. Sadly, he knew what he had to do.

He waved his arms in the air.

'I don't know – perhaps you want to live with us, secretly. Or perhaps you want to kill us. I don't think it really matters. You are our *enemies*!' He was shouting now. 'That is what you *want* to be. So I will be the Doctor, the man who *stops* enemies!'

He stepped out of the TARDIS. Clara, Rigsy and Fenton came down the ladder. Bill followed more slowly.

The green field of light was still holding the aliens back. The Doctor ran a few steps nearer to them.

'I'm sending you back to your own dimension,' he said. He opened his arms. 'Who knows? Maybe some of you will get there alive. And, if you do, remember this.' He pointed at them. 'You are not welcome here! This place is protected! I am the Doctor!'

He turned to Clara. She threw him the sonic screwdriver and he caught it. He turned to face the aliens again. Then he pointed the sonic screwdriver at them and switched it on. The green field of light pushed the aliens down the tunnel until they disappeared.

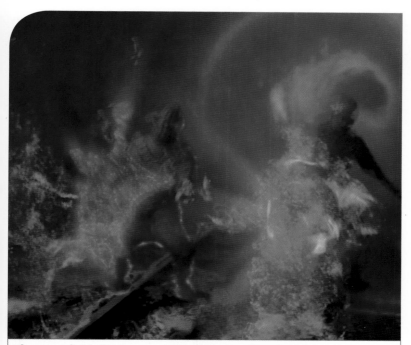

The green field of light was still holding the aliens back.

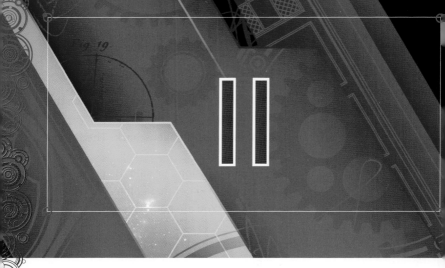

In the Sunshine

The TARDIS appeared in the same place on the same piece of empty ground at the side of the railway line, near the old railway station.

The Doctor, Clara, Fenton and Bill got out and looked around them. It was good to see the sun again. The train driver got down on his knees and kissed the ground.

Rigsy followed them out and closed the door of the TARDIS behind him. He borrowed Clara's phone and rang a number.

'Hi Mum, it's me,' he said.

Clara walked towards Bill.

'Are you all right?' she asked.

'I'm alive, and I've been inside that,' he said, pointing to the TARDIS. 'I think I'm winning. Come here.' She put her arms around him. 'Thank you,' he said.

He looked at the Doctor but the Doctor didn't smile. Bill walked away.

Clara smiled at the Doctor.

'You look happy,' he said to her. 'Are you OK?'

'I'm alive.'

'And a lot of people died,' said the Doctor, as Fenton joined them.

'But it's like a forest fire, isn't it?' Fenton said. 'You try to save the big trees, not the little ones.' He turned his head and looked at Clara. 'Am I right?' he said.

'It wasn't a fire,' said the Doctor coldly. 'Those weren't trees. Those were *people*.'

'They were criminals on Community Payback. They don't matter,' Fenton said.

He, too, turned and walked away.

The Doctor watched him go and shook his head.

'But it's good to be alive,' Fenton shouted over his shoulder. 'Thank you. Seriously, thank you.'

The Doctor looked down at the ground.

'Yes, a lot of people died and maybe the wrong people lived.'

'Yeah, but we saved the world, right?' Clara said.

'We did,' the Doctor agreed, more happily. '*You* did.'

'Yeah, well, I was *you* today. I was the Doctor,' Clara said. She looked down and stopped smiling. 'And it seems that I was quite good at it,' she said. 'You said so – when you almost died in the TARDIS.'

'You heard that, did you?' the Doctor said.

'Yeah, but the power was almost gone, so perhaps you weren't thinking clearly. You probably didn't know what you were saying.'

'Yes,' said the Doctor.

She smiled at him but he didn't smile back. The smile left her face and she looked unhappy. She didn't understand what he meant. Yes, she was a good Doctor? Or yes, he didn't know what he was saying?

Rigsy finished calling his Mum. He joined them and gave the phone back to Clara.

'Ah!' said the Doctor. 'The return of the criminal graffiti artist.'

'You do realise that he can hear you now?' Clara said.

'I know,' said the Doctor. He walked closer to Rigsy. 'Your last painting was so good that it saved the world,' he said. 'What will you do next? I can't wait to see.'

Rigsy laughed. 'It's not going to be easy,' he replied with a smile. 'I've got to be as good as a hairband.' He held out his hand to Clara. 'Thanks,' he said.

He turned and walked away.

'Your last painting was so good that it saved the world,' he said. 'What will you do next? I can't wait to see.'

Clara turned to the Doctor again. 'Say it – I did well,' she said.

Before he could answer, her phone rang. Clara looked at the screen. It was Danny. She sent a quick message and looked at the Doctor again.

'Just say it,' she told him. His back was to her now. 'Why can't you just say it?' Clara asked. 'Why can't you just say that I was good?'

The Doctor walked to the door of the TARDIS, turned and pointed at her. 'Talk to Danny,' he said.

'It's not him,' Clara said, telling a lie. She didn't want to talk to her boyfriend now. She liked Danny but she also liked her adventures on the TARDIS. It was a problem that Danny didn't want her to travel on the TARDIS. She didn't have the answer now.

She put the phone in her bag and walked towards the Doctor.

'Why can't you say it?' she repeated. 'I was the Doctor and I was good.'

'You were a very fine Doctor, Clara,' the Doctor said, finally.

'Thank you.' Clara smiled.

Activities

Chapters 1-2

Before you read

1 Look at the Word List at the back of the book. Check the meanings of words that you don't know. What are they in your language?

2 The title of this story is *Flatline*. Describe a flat line. Then find *flatline* (v) in your dictionary. What happens if a person flatlines?

3 Read In this story, at the beginning of this book. Answer these questions.

   a Where does the Doctor come from?
   b What two things does he always take with him?
   c What does the TARDIS look like?
   d What's Clara's usual job?
   e What and where does Rigsy paint?

4 Now read the Introduction to the book.

   a Where does this story happen?
   b Where exactly is the Doctor for most of the story?
   c Who is Clara?
   d When was *Doctor Who* first shown on British television?
   e Who plays the Doctor in this story?

While you read

5 Who is speaking? Write the names.

   a 'Do you need help? Sir?'

   ....

   b 'Why can't I leave even my toothbrush here?'

   ....

   c 'The TARDIS is smaller – that's really, really clever.'

   ....

   d 'It isn't often that I don't know something.'

   ....

e 'This is Community Payback, not a holiday.'

....

f 'I do graffiti. Nothing like murder or …'

....

After you read

....

6 Something strange is happening in Bristol. A man has disappeared into the floor of his flat. Other people have disappeared but we don't know where to. The TARDIS is in the wrong place and it is smaller. Who do you think is doing these things and why? Discuss your ideas with another student.

Chapters 3-4

Before you read

....

7 In Chapter 3, Clara will meet Rigsy again. What do you think will happen? Discuss these possibilities with another student.

    a She will like him and want to talk to him.
    b She will walk away because he is a criminal.
    c She will walk away because she has a boyfriend.
    d The Doctor will tell her to make friends with him.
    e The Doctor will want him to go away.
    f The Doctor will think that Rigsy can be useful.

While you read

....

8 Circle the right answers.

    a *Clara* / *The Doctor* thinks that the very small TARDIS is funny.
    b The TARDIS *always* / *never* lands on Earth with its real weight.
    c From inside the TARDIS, the Doctor *can* / *can't* hear Clara.
    d He *can* / *can't* see her.
    e Clara tells Rigsy that she *is* / *isn't* the Doctor.
    f In the flat, there seems to be a picture *hanging* / *painted* on the wall.
    g Rigsy *can* / *can't* be useful to Clara.
    h Rigsy *is* / *isn't* worried about aliens.
    i The TARDIS *takes in* / *loses* power.

After you read

9 The Doctor gets angry with Clara because she laughs at him. He gets angry again because she calls herself the Doctor. He also steals her idea that Rigsy will be useful. Why do you think Clara travels with him in the TARDIS? Do you think that she likes the Doctor? Why or why not? Discuss your ideas with another student.

Chapter 5

Before you read

10 There are notes at the bottom of pages 16 and 17, explaining MI5 and PC. Then use the Internet. Find out what MI5 and PC are short for. What are the names for these in your country?

While you read

11 Write the names. Who:

    a sees MI5 on the psychic paper? ....

    b lived in the flat? ....

    c has a new idea about the aliens? ....

    d uses the hammer first? ....

    e disappears? ....

    f are trying to understand three dimensions? ....

    g flatten the door handle? ....

    h is waiting for Clara in a park? ....

    i fall through the window? ....

After you read

12 Discuss how you can finish each sentence.

    a Rigsy takes Clara to the flat because …

    b PC Forrest believes that Clara is from MI5 because …

    c Clara can pull the big hammer from her bag because …

    d They hit the wall with the hammer because …

    e Clara says that she met the Doctor because …

f PC Forrest screams because …
g The Doctor thinks that the aliens are cutting people up because …
h Clara and Rigsy climb into the chair because …
i Clara takes the call from Danny because …
j The chair goes through the window because …

Chapters 6-7

Before you read

13 In Chapter 6 the aliens kill another person. Which of these people do you think it will be?

Clara Fenton the Doctor Stan Danny Rigsy

Discuss your ideas with other students.

While you read

14 Complete the sentences with these words.

psychic paper   sonic screwdriver   loudspeakers   finger
jackets   earphone   brushes   railway

a When Clara hears strange noises, she puts her hand to the
   …………………… .
b The Community Payback group are using paint and …………………… .
c Clara uses the …………………… to mend the earphone.
d The Doctor's …………………… comes out of her bag and points at
   the wall.
e Fenton can't see anything on the …………………… .
f Clara and the men run into a …………………… building.
g Clara climbs a ladder to reach the …………………… .
h The aliens give the numbers on the men's …………………… .

After you read

15 In these two chapters, the Doctor has some ideas. In what order
(1-6) does he have them?

   a The aliens have tried to understand people.

b The aliens are hiding in the underpass paintings.

c The missing people are in the underpass paintings.

d Painted footsteps on the underpass walls show how the aliens saw three-dimensional people.

e The aliens are from a universe with only two dimensions.

f Perhaps the aliens don't know that people need three dimensions.

Chapter 8

Before you read

....

16 All over Britain there are old railways with tunnels and bridges. Many of these have no railway lines now and are enjoyed by walkers and people on bicycles. Why do you think that Britain has so many of these old lines? Use a library or the Internet to find out.

While you read

....

17 Who is speaking? Who are they talking to? What (in *italics*) are they talking about?

a 'That's three exits all closed by *them*.'

....

....

b 'But we can't get through *it*, can we?'

....

....

c 'It's one of mine. Do you like it?'

....

....

d 'We're not calling *it* a de-flattener!'

....

....

e 'He's getting signs of *them* all around.'

....

....

f 'If *it's* flat, are we safe now?'

....

....

After you read

18 Tell other students. Answer their questions.

    a Imagine that you are Clara. The Doctor gave you the 2Dis for the first time. How did you feel? What did you do with it? What happened?

    b Imagine that you are Clara. The Doctor gave you the 2Dis for the second time. How did you feel? What did you do with it? What happened?

    c Imagine that you are Clara, the Doctor or one of the other (living) men. Describe why you were very frightened at the end of this chapter.

Chapters 9-10

Before you read

19 The TARDIS has fallen onto a railway line and a train is coming. The TARDIS can't move because it has no power. Clara has an idea. What does she tell the Doctor to do? Discuss this with another student.

While you read

20 Are these sentences right (✔) or wrong (✗)?

    a The Doctor can't help Clara now.

    b Clara and the men find themselves between the aliens and a moving train.

    c The Doctor saves the TARDIS.

    d The TARDIS has power again.

    e Bill can move his train without a driver.

    f Rigsy drives the train into the aliens.

    g Clara finds the TARDIS.

    h Clara gives Rigsy an important job.

    i The aliens think that Rigsy's painting is a real door.

    j Energy from the aliens gives power to the TARDIS.

    k The Doctor still wants to be the aliens' friend.

After you read

21 There are a number of possible actions that the Doctor can take with the aliens:

- He can destroy them in the tunnel.
- He can send them back to their own dimension.
- He can keep them in the tunnel and try to talk to them.

Which one does he choose? Why? Do you think he was right? Discuss these questions with another student.

Chapter 11

Before you read

22 Everybody is safe (or dead) now. What do you think will happen in the last chapter?

While you read

23 Write the names. Who:

  a kisses the ground? ....
  b makes a phone call? ....
  c enjoyed his trip in the TARDIS? ....
  d doesn't mind that criminals died? ....
  e has changed the Doctor's opinion of him? ....
  f really wants kind words from the Doctor? ....
  g lies to the Doctor? ....
  h finally says that Clara did well? ....

After you read

24 In this story, the Doctor is inside the TARDIS for most of the time. The writer was told that it had to be like this. Why, do you think? Discuss your ideas with another student.

Writing

25 Imagine that you were the Doctor's companion on one of his earlier journeys in the TARDIS. Where did you go? Was it in this world or another world, in the past, present or future? What happened? Write the story.

26 Imagine that you write for a local Bristol newspaper. People have started to disappear, and now an old police box has appeared. What is happening? What do people think? Write a report.

27 Do you believe in aliens? Do you think there is any life in other parts of the universe? Or are we alone? Give reasons for your opinions.

28 Rigsy is a graffiti artist. What do you think about graffiti? Is it art or are the painters criminals? Write your ideas.

29 Write the conversation between Bill and his boss after he arrives back at the railway station without his train. Will his boss believe what happened in the tunnel? Will Bill show him the two-dimensional train on the tunnel wall?

30 Clara decides that she wants to travel with the Doctor in the TARDIS again. She feels uncomfortable about telling Danny face to face. Write her email to him.

31 Write Fenton's report to his boss about what happened on that day of Community Payback. He also has to explain why some of the group won't return to their work in the underpass.

32 What does Rigsy know about the TARDIS, the sonic screwdriver and the psychic paper? Write what he tells a friend about each of these.

33 'Your last painting was so good that it saved the world,' the Doctor said. 'What will you do next? I can't wait to see.' Rigsy decides that he wants to change his life – no more graffiti, no more Community Payback. But he still wants to paint. Write a conversation between Rigsy and his mother about his plans.

34 *Doctor Who* is science fiction. Why do many people love science fiction, do you think? What kinds of books, films or TV programmes do you enjoy most, and why?

Word List

alarm (n) a piece of equipment that makes a loud noise in times of danger. A fire alarm, for example, tells you that there is a fire.

alien (n) a fictional living thing from another world.

brush (n) something that you paint or clean with.

ceiling (n) the inside part of the top of a room.

control (n) a part of a machine. You press it or turn it to make the machine work.

device (n) a machine or tool that does a special job.

dimension (n) the size of something: how long, wide, deep or high it is.

energy (n) something that makes movement possible. Energy can come from the sun, for example. Food gives people energy.

flash (v) to shine brightly for a short time and then stop shining.

graffiti (n) words or pictures that are painted on walls or trains, for example. Graffiti artists are usually breaking the law.

hairband (n) a thin piece of cloth that you use to tie your hair away from your face.

hammer (n) a tool with a heavy metal part on a long piece of wood, used for hitting things.

handle (n) the part of a door that you open it with.

poster (n) a large printed notice or picture.

power (n) the energy that is needed by a machine. The power for an electric car comes from electricity, for example.

scan (v) to check an area carefully but quickly, with your eyes or a piece of equipment. **Scanners** produce pictures of what is inside something.

screen (n) the part of a television or computer where the picture or information appears.

torch (n) a small electric light that you carry in your hand.

tunnel (n) a long hole under the ground for cars or trains, for example, to pass through.

universe (n) all of space and time and everything in it.